NO MORE SHEETS

Bynum

*Wholeness
Through
Holiness*

No More Sheets

Printed in the United States of America

Copyright © 1998 Juanita Bynum
No More Sheets - Quote Book ISBN 1-56229-154-8

Pneuma Life Publishing
P. O. Box 885
Lanham, Maryland 20703-0885
(301) 577-4052
http://www.pneumalife.com

Cover by DesignPoint Inc.

Other products by Juanita Bynum

No More Sheets (Softcover and Hardback)
No More Sheets Devotional
No More Sheets Quote Book
Morning Glory Devotional
Morning Glory Gift Book
Morning Glory Prayer Journal
Don't Get Off the Train
The Planted Seed
The Juanita Bynum Topical Bible
Prayer and Consecration
Never Mess with a Man who Came Out of a Cave - Mini Book
My Inheritance - Mini Book

Pneuma Life Publishing
P. O. Box 885
Lanham, Maryland 20703-0885
(301) 577-4052
(800) 727-3218
http://www.pneumalife.com

Juanita Bynum Ministries
Post Office Box 939
Waycross, GA 31502 U.S.A.
(912) 287-0032
(800) 979-9195
Internet: http://www.nosheets.com

Introduction

My brothers and sisters, we are in a heated battle to reclaim the respect of our human bodies. We are all vital members in the body of Christ, therefore, the stakes are so very high. We cannot afford to lose even one person from our camp.

Perhaps you were planning to just skim through a bunch of Juanita Bynum quotes ... I now interrupt your program with a message from the Emergency Bynum System:

What you are now holding is a loaded arsenal against the enemy and all his chiefs. Proceed without caution. There can be no more prisoners in this war. So come on soldier, sound the alarm ... *No More Sheets!*

WARNING: KINGDOM OF DARKNESS IRRITANT. HARMFUL TO SATAN AND ALL HIS COHORTS IF USED. THIS BOOK WILL INFLICT PERMANENT DAMAGE TO EVERY LIE THE DEVIL SHOOTS YOUR WAY TO KEEP YOU IN BONDAGE TO HIS WILL. KEEP IN REACH AT ALL TIMES.

INGREDIENTS: Common sense mixed with the most powerful weapon known to man—the awesome Word of God.

DIRECTIONS: For maximum results, read several times, commit to memory, use in the midst of opposition, annihilate the enemy, and win!

*E*veryday of your life, you must struggle to kill the flesh.

Now the works of the flesh are manifest, which are these; Adultery, fornication, uncleanness, lasciviousness, Idolatry, witchcraft, hatred, variance, emulations, wrath, strife, seditions, heresies, Envyings, murders, drunkenness, revellings, and such like: of the which I tell you before, as I have also told you in time past, that they which do such things shall not inherit the kingdom of God.
Galatians 5:19-21

Don't even fool yourself. Masturbation and pornography will never be enough to satisfy you.

But I say unto you, That whosoever looketh on a woman to lust after her hath committed adultery with her already in his heart.
Matthew 5:28

*P*honiness won't cut it. If the church doesn't get real, we're going to lose a whole lot of folks.

Take heed unto thyself, and unto the doctrine; continue in them: for in doing this thou shalt both save thyself, and them that hear thee.
1 Tim. 4:16

According to the spirit realm, you become one with each person you have sex with.

For this cause shall a man leave his father and mother, and shall be joined unto his wife, and they two shall be one flesh.
Ephes. 5:31

What are you bringing to the table besides eyeliner and lipstick?

Favour is deceitful, and beauty is vain: but a woman that feareth the LORD, she shall be praised.
Proverbs 31:30

Have you ever wondered why you're not married? You're not married because you're not single yet-you've been married too many times. Every time you have sex, you are marrying that person in the spirit.

Know ye not that your bodies are the members of Christ? shall I then take the members of Christ, and make them the members of an harlot? God forbid. What? know ye not that he which is joined to an harlot is one body? for two, saith he, shall be one flesh.
1 Cor. 6:15-16

*H*ow can you even think about getting married when you don't even know how to cook, your nails are too long to make a biscuit, you can't wash clothes, and your house is always tore up? Consider the Proverbs 31 woman:

She looketh well to the ways of her household, and eateth not the bread of idleness.
Proverbs 31:27

How can you get married when you're still in debt and can't even pay your bills? You're too needy! You're supposed to be a help-meet, not a dead-beat!

And the LORD God said, It is not good that the man should be alone; I will make him an help meet for him.
Genesis 2:18

*G*od is going to bless you according to your level of integrity.

So he fed them according to the integrity of his heart;
and guided them by the skilfulness of his hands.
Psalm 78:72

*Y*our sexy shape will not determine your level of blessing.

The LORD rewarded me according to my righteousness; according to the cleanness of my hands hath he recompensed me.
Psalm 18:20

So what somebody bought you something- buy it yourself!

They give gifts to all whores: but thou givest thy gifts to all thy lovers, and hirest them, that they may come unto thee on every side for thy whoredom.
Ezekiel 16:33

Singles ought to be the biggest givers in the church.

But I would have you without carefulness. He that is unmarried careth for the things that belong to the Lord, how he may please the Lord:
1 Cor. 7:32

*Y*our imagination can be used as a setup to entrap you.

But they hearkened not, nor inclined their ear, but walked in the counsels and in the imagination of their evil heart, and went backward, and not forward.
Jeremiah 7:24

When a no-good demon is still saying,
"Hey, Baby . . . I sure would like to get
with you," then you should examine the
way you look and dress.

*As a jewel of gold in a swine's snout, so is a fair woman
which is without discretion.*
Proverbs 11:22

To overcome, you've got to fast. You don't have a choice.

Is not this the fast that I have chosen? to loose the bands of wickedness, to undo the heavy burdens, and to let the oppressed go free, and that ye break every yoke?
Isaiah 58:6

*I*n the midst of opposition, no matter what the enemy brings your way, no matter how fine she is, no matter how good he looks-
No More Sheets!

No weapon that is formed against thee shall prosper; and every tongue that shall rise against thee in judgment thou shalt condemn. This is the heritage of the servants of the LORD, and their righteousness is of me, saith the LORD.
Isaiah 54:17

No more lies, deceit, pain, grief, abuse, or misuse. You're Free!!! No More Sheets!!!

If the Son therefore shall make you free, ye shall be free indeed.
John 8:36

*Y*ou are in a battle to regain the respect
of your body.

*What? know ye not that your body is the temple of the
Holy Ghost which is in you, which ye have of God, and
ye are not your own?*
1 Cor. 6:19

Trust God.

Trust in the LORD with all thine heart; and lean not unto thine own understanding. In all thy ways acknowledge him, and he shall direct thy paths.
Proverbs 3:5-6

The Lord should always be the ultimate joy in your life.

for the joy of the LORD is your strength."
Neh. 8:10b

*H*ave the courage to say to the Lord,
"Until you're finished processing me,
please don't send anyone my way."

*Fear thou not; for I am with thee: be not dismayed; for
I am thy God: I will strengthen thee; yea, I will thee;
yea, I will uphold thee with the right hand
of my righteousness.*
Isaiah 41:10

llow the anointing of God to close
the door on every dead relationship
you've ever had.

*How much more shall the blood of Christ, who through
the eternal Spirit offered himself without spot to God,
purge your conscience from dead works to serve
the living God?*
Hebrews 9:14

*F*rom this day forward, know that if you are enslaved, it's because you want to be, not because you have to be.

Behold, I give unto you power to tread on serpents and scorpions, and over all the power of the enemy: and nothing shall by any means hurt you.
Luke 10:19

Don't joke around and say, "I sure would like to be with that person." The enemy will get a hold of your joke and turn it into a reality.

The heart of him that hath understanding seeketh knowledge: but the mouth of fools feedeth on foolishness.
Proverbs 15:14

*D*o you know what happens when you don't keep your speech clean?

A wholesome tongue is a tree of life: but perverseness therein is a breach in the spirit.
Proverbs 15:4

houghts of someone with whips and chains, tied to a bed with go-go boots on and screaming are not thoughts that you should dwell on.

Finally, brethren, whatsoever things are true, whatsoever things are honest, whatsoever things are just, whatsoever things are pure, whatsoever things are lovely, whatsoever things are of good report; if there be any virtue, and if there be any praise, think on these things.

Philip. 4:8

ou cannot get what God has for you
when you're stuck in between the sheets.

*Flee fornication. Every sin that a man doeth is without
the body; but he that committeth fornication sinneth
against his own body.*
1 Cor. 6:18

*I*t is your duty to fight your flesh.
It is your duty to win.

Fight the good fight of faith, lay hold on eternal life,
whereunto thou art also called, and hast professed a
good profession before many witnesses.
1 Tim. 6:12

*I*t may not be easy, but you've got to wait on the Lord.

But they that wait upon the LORD shall renew their strength; they shall mount up with wings as eagles; they shall run, and not be weary; and they shall walk, and not faint.
Isaiah 40:31

Let go of your past and your failures.

Fear not; for thou shalt not be ashamed: neither be thou confounded; for thou shalt not be put to shame: for thou shalt forget the shame of thy youth, and shalt not remember the reproach of thy widowhood any more. For thy Maker is thine husband; the LORD of hosts is his name; and thy Redeemer the Holy One of Israel; The God of the whole earth shall he be called.
Isaiah 54:4-5

*Y*ou're not a cheap thrill. Your purpose must be fulfilled; therefore, stay still until you know God's perfect will.

Who hath saved us, and called us with an holy calling, not according to our works, but according to his own purpose and grace, which was given us in Christ Jesus before the world began,
2 Tim. 1:9

*Y*ou not only have to forgive others,
but you must also forgive yourself.
Don't allow condemnation to
eat away at you.

*There is therefore now no condemnation to them which
are in Christ Jesus, who walk not after the flesh,
but after the Spirit.*
Romans 8:1

$\mathcal{Y}$ou are complete in God, not man.

And ye are complete in him, which is the head of all principality and power:
Col. 2:10

Being alone is not the same as being lonely.

and yet I am not alone, because the Father is with me.
John 16:32b

The Lord is fed up with people being comfortable in their lustful ways.

For all that is in the world, the lust of the flesh, and the lust of the eyes, and the pride of life, is not of the Father, but is of the world. 17And the world passeth away, and the lust thereof: but he that doeth the will of God abideth for ever.
1 John 2:16-17

To be more than a conqueror in Christ, unmarried couples need to refrain and restrain themselves.

But if they cannot contain, let them marry: for it is better to marry than to burn.
1 Cor. 7:9

*E*ven when you feel weak, God is still there.

I know thy works: behold, I have set before thee an open door, and no man can shut it: for thou hast a little strength, and hast kept my word, and hast not denied my name.
Rev. 3:8

*I*niquity is doing a thing the wrong way, illegally, and without God in it.

But when the righteous turneth away from his righteousness, and committeth iniquity, and doeth according to all the abominations that the wicked man doeth, shall he live? All his righteousness that he hath done shall not be mentioned: in his trespass that he hath trespassed, and in his sin that he hath sinned, in them shall he die.

Ezekiel 18:24

The opposite of God is the devil-there is no in between.

"He that committeth sin is of the devil; for the devil sinneth from the beginning. For this purpose the Son of God was manifested, that he might destroy the works of the devil.
1 John 3:8

*A*ll of the vows you made to God at the altar must be fulfilled in order for you to be completely free.

If a man vow a vow unto the Lord, or swear an oath to bind his soul with a bond; he shall not break his word, he shall do according to all that proceedeth out of his mouth.

Numbers 30:2

The proper method to receive anything from God is through prayer and supplication.

Be careful for nothing; but in every thing by prayer and supplication with thanksgiving let your requests be made known unto God.

Philip. 4:6

*G*od can turn your every mistake into a ministry and testimony.

And all things are of God, who hath reconciled us to himself by Jesus Christ, and hath given to us the ministry of reconciliation;
2 Cor. 5:18

*J*ust because you have made a mistake doesn't mean that everything is over.

Though he fall, he shall not be utterly cast down: for the LORD upholdeth him with his hand.

Psalm 37:24

Recognize and heed the caution signs that lead to your highway of disaster.

Take heed, brethren, lest there be in any of you an evil heart of unbelief, in departing from the living God.
Hebrews 3:12

Your flesh is never exempt from temptation.

There hath no temptation taken you but such as is common to man: but God is faithful, who will not suffer you to be tempted above that ye are able; but will with the temptation also make a way to escape, that ye may be able to bear it.

1 Cor. 10:13

*J*ust because you are standing today
doesn't mean that you might
not fall tomorrow.

*Watch ye and pray, lest ye enter into temptation. The
spirit truly is ready, but the flesh is weak.*
Mark 14:38

The very second that you let your guard down you may as well expect a hit.

But know this, that if the goodman of the house had known in what watch the thief would come, he would have watched, and would not have suffered his house to be broken up.
Matthew 24:43

*T*emptation is not wrong. Yielding to temptation is wrong.

But every man is tempted, when he is drawn away of his own lust, and enticed. Then when lust hath conceived, it bringeth forth sin: and sin, when it is finished, bringeth forth death.
James 1:14-15

The devil tricks many into thinking that just because they want to do it, then they ought to just go ahead and do it.

Blessed is the man that endureth temptation: for when he is tried, he shall receive the crown of life, which the Lord hath promised to them that love him.
James 1:12

Temptation is designed to test the strength of your resistance. It doesn't mean that you automatically fail just because you were given the test.

My brethren, count it all joy when ye fall into divers temptations; Knowing this, that the trying of your faith worketh patience.
James 1:2-3

When you start feeding yourself the Word of God, you can handle any test that the devil sends your way.

And Jesus answered him, saying, It is written, That man shall not live by bread alone, but by every word of God.
Luke 4:4

The Spirit of Truth living in you can stand up and attack any seducing spirit.

Howbeit when he, the Spirit of truth, is come, he will guide you into all truth: for he shall not speak of himself; but whatsoever he shall hear, that shall he speak: and he will show you things to come.
John 16:13

Fondling is not innocent. It ignites your desire to have sex.

Mortify therefore your members which are upon the earth; fornication, uncleanness, inordinate affection, evil concupiscence, and covetousness, which is idolatry:
Col. 3:5

*I*t doesn't matter how saved you are-being in the wrong places at the wrong times, late at night is just wrong.

Abstain from all appearance of evil.
1 Thes. 5:22

*T*hose that embrace a "gold-digger" mentality will stoop to all-time lows.

For by means of a whorish woman a man is brought to a piece of bread: and the adulteress will hunt for the precious life.
Proverbs 6:26

When you have no direction,
any road will do.

*Ponder the path of thy feet, and let all thy ways be
established. Turn not to the right hand nor to the left:
remove thy foot from evil.*
Proverbs 4:26-27

*I*f you are not married-to each other-then don't touch each other.

Now concerning the things whereof ye wrote unto me: It is good for a man not to touch a woman. Nevertheless, to avoid fornication, let every man have his own wife, and let every woman have her own husband.
1 Cor. 7:1-2

Your discernment will be off until you are purged and purified.

Then shall ye return, and discern between the righteous and the wicked, between him that serveth God and him that serveth him not.
Malachi 3:18

*Y*our level of maturity in God is not in years-it's in your "Yes, Lord".

For not the hearers of the law are just before God, but the doers of the law shall be justified.
Romans 2:13

*G*od doesn't come to purify your emotions. He purifies your heart in order that your spirit may control your emotions.

Draw nigh to God, and he will draw nigh to you. Cleanse your hands, ye sinners; and purify your hearts, ye double minded.
James 4:8

*I*f you can't give God your money, then it'll be harder to give Him your life.

It is easier for a camel to go through the eye of a needle, than for a rich man to enter into the kingdom of God.
Mark 10:25

*D*on't wait until tomorrow . . . come out of the sheets today.

Seek ye the LORD while he may be found, call ye upon him while he is near: Let the wicked forsake his way, and the unrighteous man his thoughts: and let him return unto the LORD, and he will have mercy upon him; and to our God, for he will abundantly pardon.
Isaiah 55:6-7

*A*llow the Lord to heal your
broken heart.

*He healeth the broken in heart, and bindeth
up their wounds.*
Psalm 147:3

*D*id you really mean it when you told the Lord, "I'm sorry"? Or, were you only sorry because you got hurt?

For I will declare mine iniquity; I will be sorry for my sin.
Psalm 38:18

Do you really love the Lord?

If ye love me, keep my commandments.
John 14:15

Have you wandered away from your vows to the Lord?

For of old time I have broken thy yoke, and burst thy bands; and thou saidst, I will not transgress; when upon every high hill and under every green tree thou wanderest, playing the harlot.
Jeremiah 2:20

When you return to things that are ungodly, you are only returning to what is still in your spirit.

As a dog returneth to his vomit, so a fool returneth to his folly.
Proverbs 26:11

*A*ny relationship that offends the Holy Spirit is not birthed through the Spirit of God.

And grieve not the holy Spirit of God, whereby ye are sealed unto the day of redemption.
Ephes. 4:30

The only person that can encourage you to keep moving towards your deliverance is someone that has the same goal; therefore, watch the company that you keep.

Iron sharpeneth iron; so a man sharpeneth the countenance of his friend.
Proverbs 27:17

*W*hen you have a reprobate mind, you exchange the truth for a lie.

And even as they did not like to retain God in their knowledge, God gave them over to a reprobate mind, to do those things which are not convenient;
Romans 1:28

Beware of the consequences of sin.

For the wages of sin is death; but the gift of God is eternal life through Jesus Christ our Lord.
Romans 6:23

*Y*ou must protect your purification
and your position in God.

Who gave himself for us, that he might redeem us from
all iniquity, and purify unto himself a peculiar people,
zealous of good works.
Titus 2:14

*J*ustification means that you have
been acquitted.

*Who shall lay any thing to the charge of God's elect? It
is God that justifieth.*
Romans 8:33

*S*anctification means that you've been set aside to serve the Lord.

And the very God of peace sanctify you wholly; and I pray God your whole spirit and soul and body be preserved blameless unto the coming of our Lord Jesus Christ.
1 Thes. 5:23

*Y*ou are not born holy. You are made holy.

Behold, I was shapen in iniquity; and in sin did my mother conceive me.
Psalm 51:5

*Y*our body must submit itself to the fact that you now hunger and thirst for righteousness.

But I keep under my body, and bring it into subjection: lest that by any means, when I have preached to others, I myself should be a castaway.

1 Cor. 9:27

*Y*ou can conquer your sheets.

Nay, in all these things we are more than conquerors through him that loved us. For I am persuaded, that neither death, nor life, nor angels, nor principalities, nor powers, nor things present, nor things to come, Nor height, nor depth, nor any other creature, shall be able to separate us from the love of God, which is in Christ Jesus our Lord.
Romans 8:37-39

People who are without understanding are covenant-breakers.

Without understanding, covenantbreakers, without natural affection, implacable, unmerciful: Who knowing the judgment of God, that they which commit such things are worthy of death, not only do the same, but have pleasure in them that do them.
Romans 1:31-32

When Satan's devices are at work,
refuse to be used.

Lest Satan should get an advantage of us: for we are not ignorant of his devices.
2 Cor. 2:11

*Y*our relationship with leadership tests your ability to be led by the Spirit of the Lord.

Obey them that have the rule over you, and submit yourselves; for they watch for your souls, as they that must give account, that they may do it with joy, and not with grief:

ride is such a strong spirit that it doesn't allow you to admit when you're hurting or feeling rejected.

Pride goeth before destruction, and an haughty spirit before a fall.
Proverbs 16:18

*S*ometimes you're so fragile and fragmented that the only thing keeping the enemy from taking a stronghold in your life is your pastor or leader.

For he is the minister of God to thee for good. But if thou do that which is evil, be afraid; for he beareth not the sword in vain: for he is the minister of God, a revenger to execute wrath upon him that doeth evil.
Romans 13:4

*I*f you are inhibited or afraid of taking someone to meet your leader or pastor, then that person is not in God's will for your life.

And I will give you pastors according to mine heart, which shall feed you with knowledge and understanding.
Jeremiah 3:15

Seek counsel when considering a potential date. Ask yourself, "Why do I want to date this person? What need do I have that this person can fulfill? Can this person encourage me to go to my next level in God? Can this person pray me through?"

Hear counsel, and receive instruction, that thou mayest be wise in thy latter end. There are many devices in a man's heart; nevertheless the counsel of the LORD, that shall stand.
Proverbs 19:20-21

Research your dates. Make sure that they walk in integrity, haven't left any scars behind, and haven't wounded anyone.

The way of a fool is right in his own eyes: but he that hearkeneth unto counsel is wise.
Proverbs 12:15

*W*hen it gets rough, always remember that
God is in control.

*Be strong and of a good courage, fear not, nor be afraid
of them: for the LORD thy God, he it is that doth go
with thee; he will not fail thee, nor forsake thee.*
Deut. 31:6

"*Lord, let your will be done in my life.*"

"*And he said, Abba, Father, all things are possible*
unto thee; take away this cup from me:
nevertheless not what I will,
but what thou wilt."
Mark 14:36

Don't give any place to the devil to draw you back into sin.

Neither give place to the devil.
Ephes. 4:27

As long as the enemy and what he has is greater and more valuable to you than God, then you will never embrace what God has for you.

Ye are of God, little children, and have overcome them: because greater is he that is in you, than he that is in the world.
1 John 4:4

Humble yourself before the Lord.

Humble yourselves in the sight of the Lord,
and he shall lift you up.
James 4:10

When operating in witchcraft-which includes rebellion-everything you touch crumbles, no doors can be opened for you properly, and you are headed for a fall.

For rebellion is as the sin of witchcraft, and stubbornness is as iniquity and idolatry. Because thou hast rejected the word of the LORD, he hath also rejected thee from being king.
1 Samuel 15:23

*G*od cares for all that repent and turn their hearts to Him.

Repent ye therefore, and be converted, that your sins may be blotted out, when the times of refreshing shall come from the presence of the Lord;
Acts 3:19

You are reading this book because it's your season-it's your turn. God will not let the enemy devour your life.

And I will rebuke the devourer for your sakes, and he shall not destroy the fruits of your ground; neither shall your vine cast her fruit before the time in the field, saith the LORD of hosts.
Malachi 3:11

I prophesy to you, "The Lord is in control of your life. Fear not. What the enemy meant for your harm, the Lord is turning things around for your good."

But as for you, ye thought evil against me; but God meant it unto good, to bring to pass, as it is this day, to save much people alive.
Genesis 50:20

*E*very detail of your life will work together
for your good.

*And we know that all things work together for good to
them that love God, to them who are the called
according to his purpose.*
Romans 8:28

You cannot afford to live a borderline life.

I know thy works, that thou art neither cold nor hot: I would thou wert cold or hot. So then because thou art lukewarm, and neither cold nor hot, I will spue thee out of my mouth.
Rev. 3:15-16

*P*ut away your former conversation—
stop talking about sex and foolishness.

That ye put off concerning the former conversation the old man, which is corrupt according to the deceitful lusts; And be renewed in the spirit of your mind; And that ye put on the new man, which after God is created in righteousness and true holiness. Wherefore putting away lying, speak every man truth with his neighbour: for we are members one of another.
Ephes. 4:22-25

*R*emembering your struggles and victories helps to keep you conscious of who you are and what you are doing.

Remember therefore from whence thou art fallen, and repent, and do the first works; or else I will come unto thee quickly, and will remove thy candlestick out of his place, except thou repent.

Rev. 2:5

*D*ecree now, "No More Sheets! No More Sheets! No More Sheets!"

2:5 Thou shalt also decree a thing, and it shall be established unto thee: and the light shall shine upon thy ways.
Job 22:28

*D*on't give up. If I can make it,
you can make it.

Let us hold fast the profession of our faith without wavering; (for he is faithful that promised;)
Hebrews 10:23

*O*ne of the most powerful tools you can use is your ability to testify.

And they overcame him by the blood of the Lamb, and by the word of their testimony; and they loved not their lives unto the death.
Rev. 12:11

*M*any people hide their secrets and sufferings behind fake smiles.

Even so ye also outwardly appear righteous unto men, but within ye are full of hypocrisy and iniquity.
Matthew 23:28

Unleash your battle cry against promiscuity, adultery, pornography, and incest by declaring that there will be NO MORE SHEETS!

What shall we then say to these things? If God be for us, who can be against us?
Romans 8:31

*D*on't even think about slipping back into your old ways—you know better.

The backslider in heart shall be filled with his own ways: and a good man shall be satisfied from himself.
Proverbs 14:14

roken promises from those you've been with will steal a piece of your soul.

A merry heart doeth good like a medicine: but a broken spirit drieth the bones.
Proverbs 17:22

When searching for love in all the wrong places, you'll only find masks hiding deceitful faces.

Bread of deceit is sweet to a man; but afterwards his mouth shall be filled with gravel.
Proverbs 20:17

Men are not dogs—that terminology offends the very essence of God.

So God created man in his own image, in the image of God created he him; male and female created he them.
Genesis 1:27

A modern day Delilah is a woman who is more interested in what's in your pants than what's in your heart, mind, and spirit.

For the lips of a strange woman drop as an honeycomb, and her mouth is smoother than oil: But her end is bitter as wormwood, sharp as a twoedged sword. Her feet go down to death; her steps take hold on hell.
Proverbs 5:3-5

*D*on't even pretend like you're Peter Pan or Tinkerbell in the Body of Christ-so strong in every area of your life and flying so high in the spirit that your feet never touch the ground.

Watch and pray, that ye enter not into temptation: the spirit indeed is willing, but the flesh is weak.
Matthew 26:41

*I*f you just want a diamond ring and a beautiful white dress, then go buy them for yourself and the next time your church has a banquet, wear your white dress with your ring; however, don't let these be your motivation for getting married.

A good name is rather to be chosen than great riches,
and loving favour rather than silver and gold.
Proverbs 22:1

Circumcision was done as a covenant. The only woman who is to experience your circumcised ring should be wearing your wedding ring.

And ye shall circumcise the flesh of your foreskin; and it shall be a token of the covenant betwixt me and you.
Genesis 17:11

When you discipline yourself, your spirit rules your flesh.

This I say then, Walk in the Spirit, and ye shall not fulfil the lust of the flesh.
Galatians 5:16

Bitterness doesn't destroy anybody but yourself.

Looking diligently lest any man fail of the grace of God; lest any root of bitterness springing up trouble you, and thereby many be defiled;
Hebrews 12:15

*G*od is not going to leave you in the state you're in. Victory is yours!!

But thanks be to God, which giveth us the victory through our Lord Jesus Christ.
1 Cor. 15:57

Once you've been released from bondage, why do you still want the chains? Once freed from slavery, why would you still want the shackles? Get rid of everything that represents the bondage you were in— i.e., clothes, jewelry, furniture, etc.

And thou shalt gather all the spoil of it into the midst of the street thereof, and shalt burn with fire the city, and all the spoil thereof every whit, for the LORD thy God: and it shall be an heap for ever; it shall not be built again.
Deut. 13:16

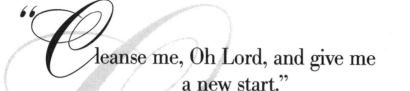

"Cleanse me, Oh Lord, and give me a new start."

Behold, I will do a new thing; now it shall spring forth;
shall ye not know it? I will even make a way in the
wilderness, and rivers in the desert.
Isaiah 43:19

*A*fter 12:00 midnight, ain't nothing open but legs!!!

Woe unto them that seek deep to hide their counsel from the LORD, and their works are in the dark, and they say, Who seeth us? and who knoweth us?
Isaiah 29:15

Pornography is not harmless. It gets into your spirit and awakens your appetite to fornicate.

Thou art of purer eyes than to behold evil, and canst not look on iniquity: wherefore lookest thou upon them that deal treacherously, and holdest thy tongue when the wicked devoureth the man that is more righteous than he?
Habakkuk 1:13

Guard your heart.

Keep thy heart with all diligence; for out of it are the issues of life.
Proverbs 4:23

"*I* need a prophecy. I need a prophet." No . . . you need a Bible! Hear Him through His Word.

For the word of God is living and active. Sharper than any double-edged sword, it penetrates even to dividing soul and spirit, joints and marrow; it judges the thoughts and attitudes of the heart.
Hebrews 4:12

"**You** need to be in a church.

Not forsaking the assembling of ourselves together, as the manner of some is; but exhorting one another: and so much the more, as ye see the day approaching.
Hebrews 10:25

*G*od is calling us to prayer, consecration, and santification.

Pray without ceasing.
1 Thes. 5:17

*Y*ou don't just wake up one day in the sheets-there is a process in, and there is a process out.

My people are destroyed for lack of knowledge: because thou hast rejected knowledge, I will also reject thee, that thou shalt be no priest to me: seeing thou hast forgotten the law of thy God, I will also forget thy children.

Hosea 4:6

Disconnect yourself from those who try to draw you away from the will of God.

Now I beseech you, brethren, mark them which cause divisions and offences contrary to the doctrine which ye have learned; and avoid them. For they that are such serve not our Lord Jesus Christ, but their own belly; and by good words and fair speeches deceive the hearts of the simple.
Romans 16:17-18

*I*f you know the Lord and you still do not glorify Him, you will often find yourself in a mess.

For if after they have escaped the pollutions of the world through the knowledge of the Lord and Saviour Jesus Christ, they are again entangled therein, and overcome, the latter end is worse with them than the beginning. For it had been better for them not to have known the way of righteousness, than, after they have known it, to turn from the holy commandment delivered unto them. But it is happened unto them according to the true proverb, The dog is turned to his own vomit again; and the sow that was washed to her wallowing in the mire.

2 Peter 2:20-22

*D*on't allow your mind to be open to the spirit of your past.

And be not conformed to this world: but be ye transformed by the renewing of your mind, that ye may prove what is that good, and acceptable, and perfect, will of God.
Romans 12:2

When the enemy can't use a person to physically seduce you, he tries to mentally seduce you through what you hear and see.

Be sober, be vigilant; because your adversary the devil, as a roaring lion, walketh about, seeking whom he may devour:
1 Peter 5:8

Desperate for love, many compromise by thinking, "Well, as long as he treats me nice, I really don't care if he's saved."

Be ye not unequally yoked together with unbelievers: for what fellowship hath righteousness with unrighteousness? and what communion hath light with darkness?
2 Cor. 6:14

When you say, "Lord, help me," the Spirit takes the Word and lifts up a standard against the devil.

So shall they fear the name of the LORD from the west, and his glory from the rising of the sun. When the enemy shall come in like a flood, the Spirit of the LORD shall lift up a standard against him.
Isaiah 59:19

*I*f you are like me, you want to hear "hold on" from someone who is really holding on.

For we have not an high priest which cannot be touched with the feeling of our infirmities; but was in all points tempted like as we are, yet without sin.
Hebrews 4:15

*F*or too long, we have hid behind what we are supposed to be instead of being who we really are. Superman is dead. Will some of the real Clark Kents please stand up?

If we say that we have no sin, we deceive ourselves, and the truth is not in us.
1 John 1:8

Brothers, the word "findeth" doesn't mean you try everyone out and then choose one of them. You need to wait on the Lord, and when He shows who your wife is, that's the one you choose-without leaving any damage behind.

Whoso findeth a wife findeth a good thing, and obtaineth favour of the LORD.
Proverbs 18:22

Women wonder, "What am I supposed to do while waiting for my husband to find me?" You're supposed to be obtaining the favor of the Lord as well. While you're finding God, His favor will be shining on you.

For whoso findeth me findeth life, and shall obtain favour of the LORD.
Proverbs 8:35

We play sisterhood so cheap. Instead of being in competition for the men in our churches, let's help each other get out and stay out of the sheets.

For if they fall, the one will lift up his fellow: but woe to him that is alone when he falleth; for he hath not another to help him up.
Eccles. 4:10

How often do you turn to God in worship, prayer, and meditation? Do you read the Word more than once a day? If you're like a lot of Christians, you're malnourished.

This book of the law shall not depart out of thy mouth; but thou shalt meditate therein day and night, that thou mayest observe to do according to all that is written therein: for then thou shalt make thy way prosperous, and then thou shalt have good success.
Joshua 1:8

When you buy things for yourself, you can hold your head up and walk with pride because you didn't have to sleep with anyone to get them. All you paid was cash.

The blessing of the LORD, it maketh rich, and he addeth no sorrow with it.
Proverbs 10:22

I got news for you, honey. The sheets will blind you to the truth. Once you're single in heart and single in purpose, it's amazing what you'll see-you'll thank God for rescuing you!

In whom the god of this world hath blinded the minds of them which believe not, lest the light of the glorious gospel of Christ, who is the image of God, should shine unto them.
2 Cor. 4:4

When you think about an ex all of the time, remembering the scent of their perfume or cologne, or how good that person was between the sheets, you need to realize that the devil is setting you up.

Casting down imaginations, and every high thing that exalteth itself against the knowledge of God, and bringing into captivity every thought to the obedience of Christ;
2 Cor. 10:5

*M*asturbation: The bait that the devil uses to master you. Satan laughs and says, "I got you so hooked that I no longer need somebody to bring you down. I can send you to hell with the spirit of your mind. I can cause you death by your own hands."

But I see another law in my members, warring against the law of my mind, and bringing me into captivity to the law of sin which is in my members. O wretched man that I am! who shall deliver me from the body of this death? I thank God through Jesus Christ our Lord. So then with the mind I myself serve the law of God; but with the flesh the law of sin.
Romans 7:23-25

If you were bound by masturbation, and you heard Jesus preach that day, what would you think?

And if thy right hand offend thee, cut if off, and cast it from thee: for it is profitable for thee that one of thy members should perish, and not that thy whole body should be cast into hell.
Matthew 5:30

You have a decision to make. Are you going to meet your own needs, or are you going to ask God to send a mate to meet those needs? It's up to you.

Be not ye therefore like unto them: for your Father knoweth what things ye have need of, before ye ask him.
Matthew 6:8

But my God shall supply all your need according to his riches in glory by Christ Jesus.
Philip. 4:19

Many times people choose a mate who can rock their world right now. God chooses a mate who can satisfy where they're going. God knows the best person to help you fulfill your calling.

The eyes of your understanding being enlightened; that ye may know what is the hope of his calling, and what the riches of the glory of his inheritance in the saints,
Ephes. 1:18

*I*f we allowed God to be our matchmaker, there would be less divorce in the church, more compatibility in marriages, and a greater fulfillment of His purposes on the earth-God knows what is down the road for you.

I am Alpha and Omega, the beginning and the end, the first and the last.
Rev. 22:13

*I*sn't it interesting that we know what it takes to shape up our bodies, but we're clueless when it comes to forming our character?

And beside this, giving all diligence, add to your faith virtue; and to virtue knowledge; And to knowledge temperance; and to temperance patience; and to patience godliness; And to godliness brotherly kindness; and to brotherly kindness charity. For if these things be in you, and abound, they make you that ye shall neither be barren nor unfruitful in the knowledge of our Lord Jesus Christ.
2 Peter 1:5-8

Take your time in any relationship. Once you're married, you'll have the rest of your lives together. The most important issue while you're still single is to make a wise choice.

"O that they were wise, that they understood this, that they would consider their latter end!
Deut. 32:29

Some woman will spend hundreds of
dollars to get a man's thousands.
When a woman is more concerned about
your bank book than your expectations,
drop her as fast as you can.

*And I find more bitter than death the woman, whose
heart is snares and nets, and her hands as bands:
whoso pleaseth God shall escape from her; but the
sinner shall be taken by her.*
Eccles. 7:26

*M*en, look for character-not just outer beauty. Far too many decisions are made with hormones and not a heart submitted to the wisdom of the Lord.

A virtuous woman is a crown to her husband: but she that maketh ashamed is as rottenness in his bones.
Proverbs 12:4

*M*en, there is a penalty to be paid
for misguided erections. Sex with a woman
who is not your spouse will sap your
strength. If you keep losing your strength,
eventually you will die. If you're dead to
God, you won't fulfill your destiny.

Give not thy strength unto women, nor thy ways to that
which destroyeth kings.
Proverbs 31:3

"*Sheets*" are layers of bondage that have affected your emotions through sexual experiences. If you want to enjoy the fullness of God, you must cast off those sheets and declare for every future relationship, "No More Sheets!"

That he would grant you, according to the riches of his glory, to be strengthened with might by his Spirit in the inner man; That Christ may dwell in your hearts by faith; that ye, being rooted and grounded in love, May be able to comprehend with all saints what is the breadth, and length, and depth, and height; And to know the love of Christ, which passeth knowledge, that ye might be filled with all the fulness of God.
Ephes. 3:16-19

Sisters are carrying around the baggage of past relationships and sexual encounters. Brothers aren't free to answer God's call on their lives. Weighed down with guilt, shame, and regret, these believers have become ineffective for the kingdom of God.

Come unto me, all ye that labour and are heavy laden, and I will give you rest. Take my yoke upon you, and learn of me; for I am meek and lowly in heart: and ye shall find rest unto your souls. For my yoke is easy, and my burden is light.
Matthew 11:28-30

You might be living right, but if you're flipping through the channels and watching sex acts, you are being enticed and drawn away by your own lust.

Let no man say when he is tempted, I am tempted of God: for God cannot be tempted with evil, neither tempteth he any man: But every man is tempted, when he is drawn away of his own lust, and enticed.
James 1:13-14

*S*top blaming others. You need to explore what it is about you that may not be right.

Search me, O God, and know my heart: try me, and know my thoughts:
Psalm 139:23

Purge means to make clean. Purge means to cleanse harshly.

But who may abide the day of his coming? and who shall stand when he appeareth? for he is like a refiner's fire, and like fullers' sope: And he shall sit as a refiner and purifier of silver: and he shall purify the sons of Levi, and purge them as gold and silver, that they may offer unto the LORD an offering in righteousness.
Malachi 3:2-3

When your lifestyle and deeds don't reflect your salvation, the only one that knows you're saved is you.

Ye are the light of the world. A city that is set on an hill cannot be hid. Neither do men light a candle, and put it under a bushel, but on a candlestick; and it giveth light unto all that are in the house. Let your light so shine before men, that they may see your good works, and glorify your Father which is in heaven.
Matthew 5:14-16

Whenever you claim deliverance,
you'd better be ready to be confronted
in that area.

*But sanctify the Lord God in your hearts: and be
ready always to give an answer to every man that
asketh you a reason of the hope that is in you
with meekness and fear:*
1 Peter 3:15